Organs!
Vital Human Organs
(Brain, Heart, Kidneys, Liver and Lungs)
Children's Biology Books

Copyright 2016

All Rights reserved. No part of this book may be reproduced or used in any way or form or by any means whether electronic or mechanical, this means that you cannot record or photocopy any material ideas or tips that are provided in this book

What makes us alive? What keeps us breathing?

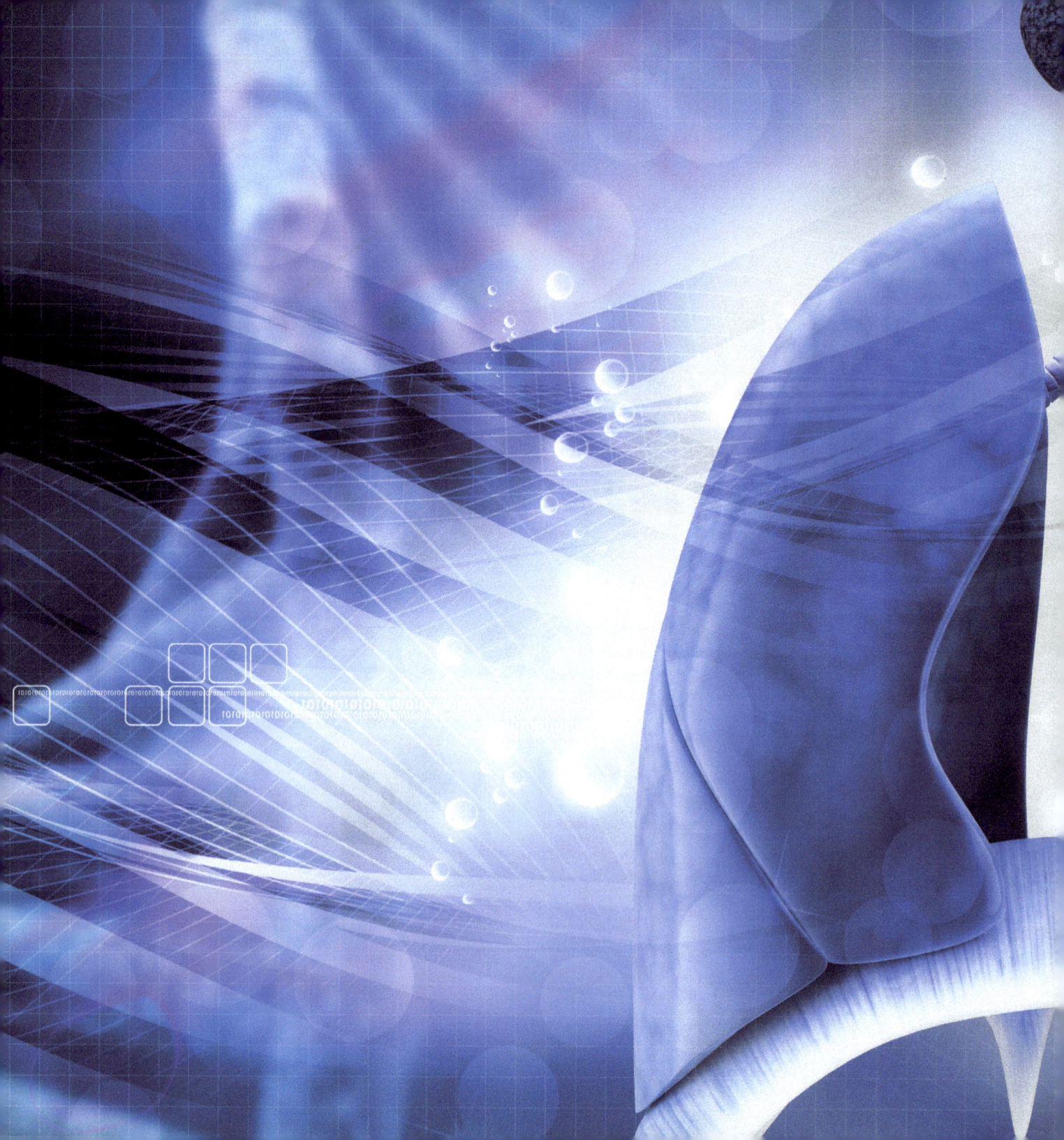

Just like all animals on the Earth, we as humans have vital organs that keep us going every day!

Our vital organs are exceptionally important! They have functions that sustain our lives.

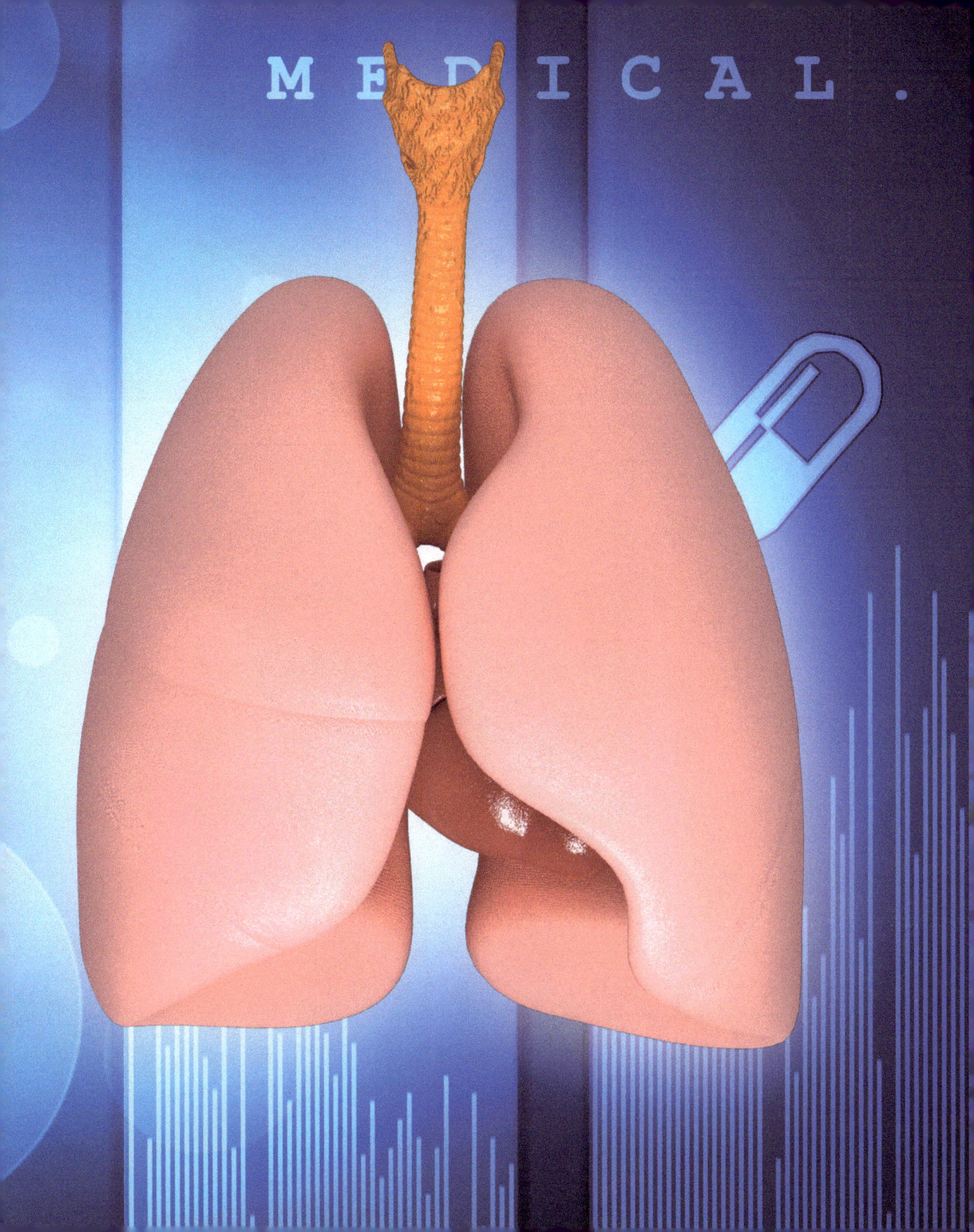

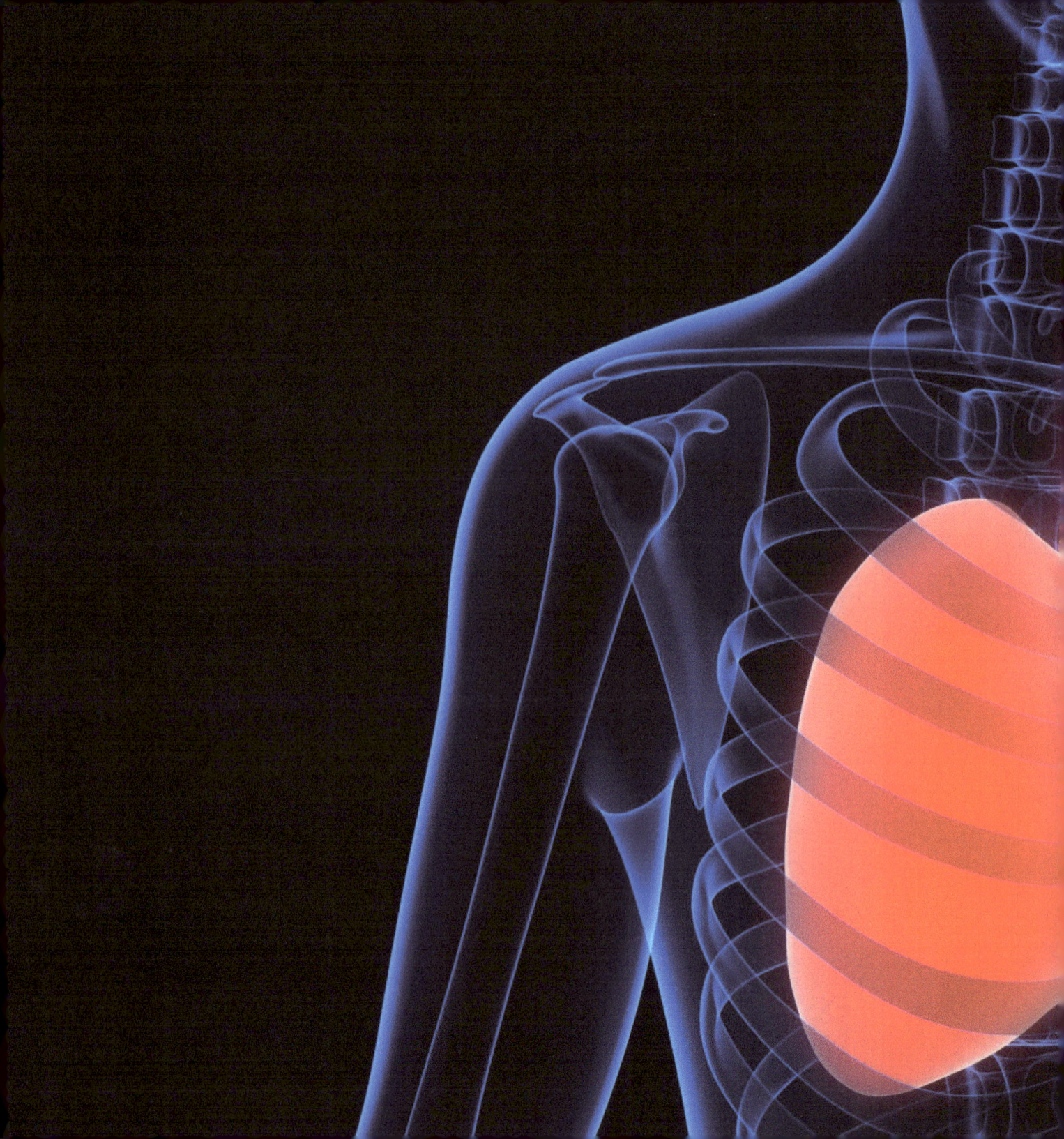

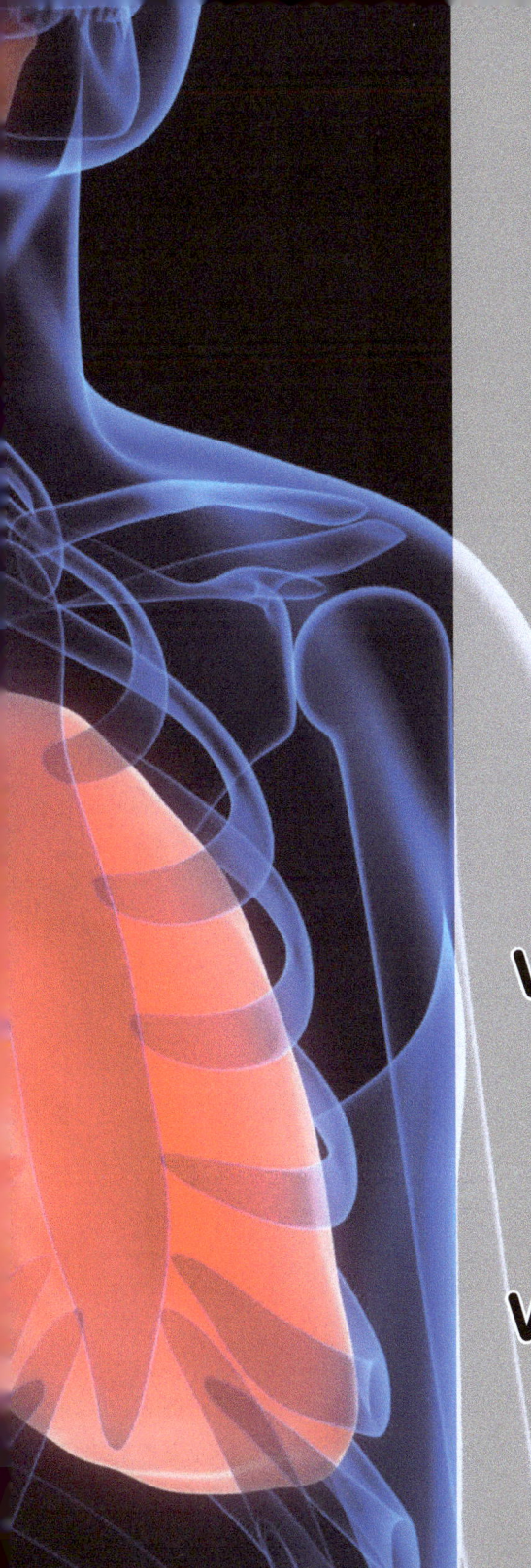

Let's learn more about our vital organs. Learning their functions will encourage us to treat them well with a healthy lifestyle. Keep them healthy, so we can live longer!

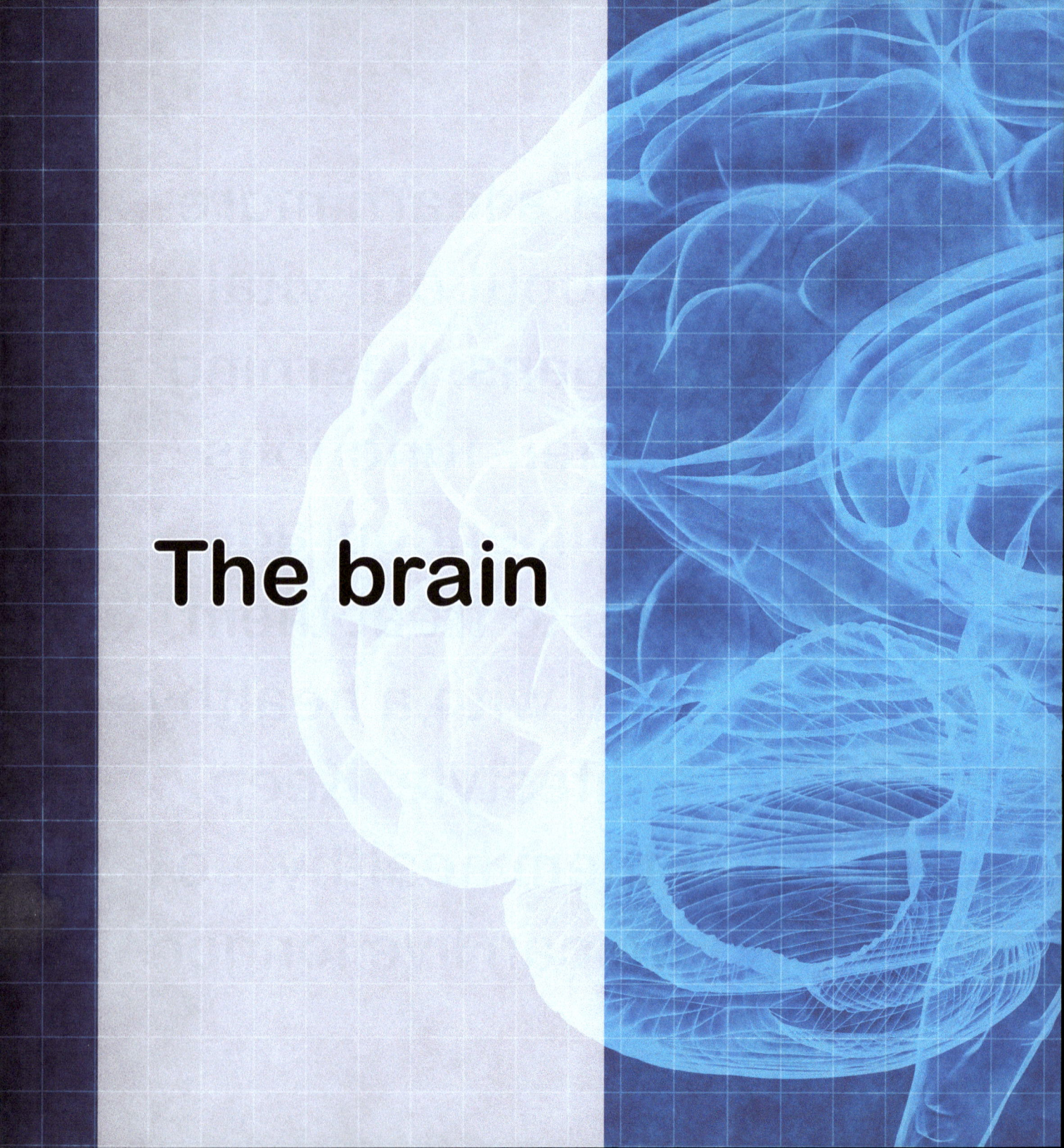
The brain

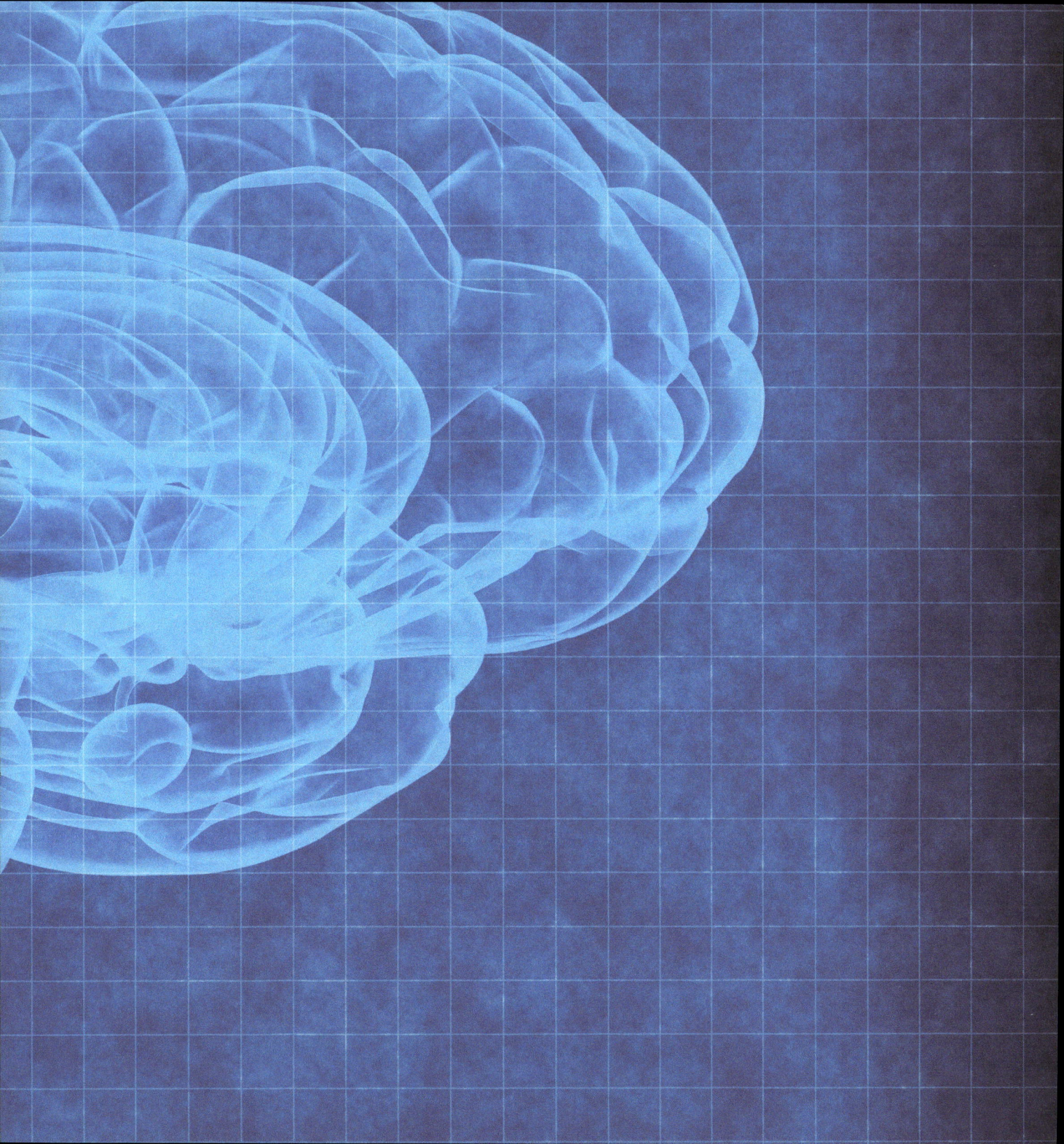

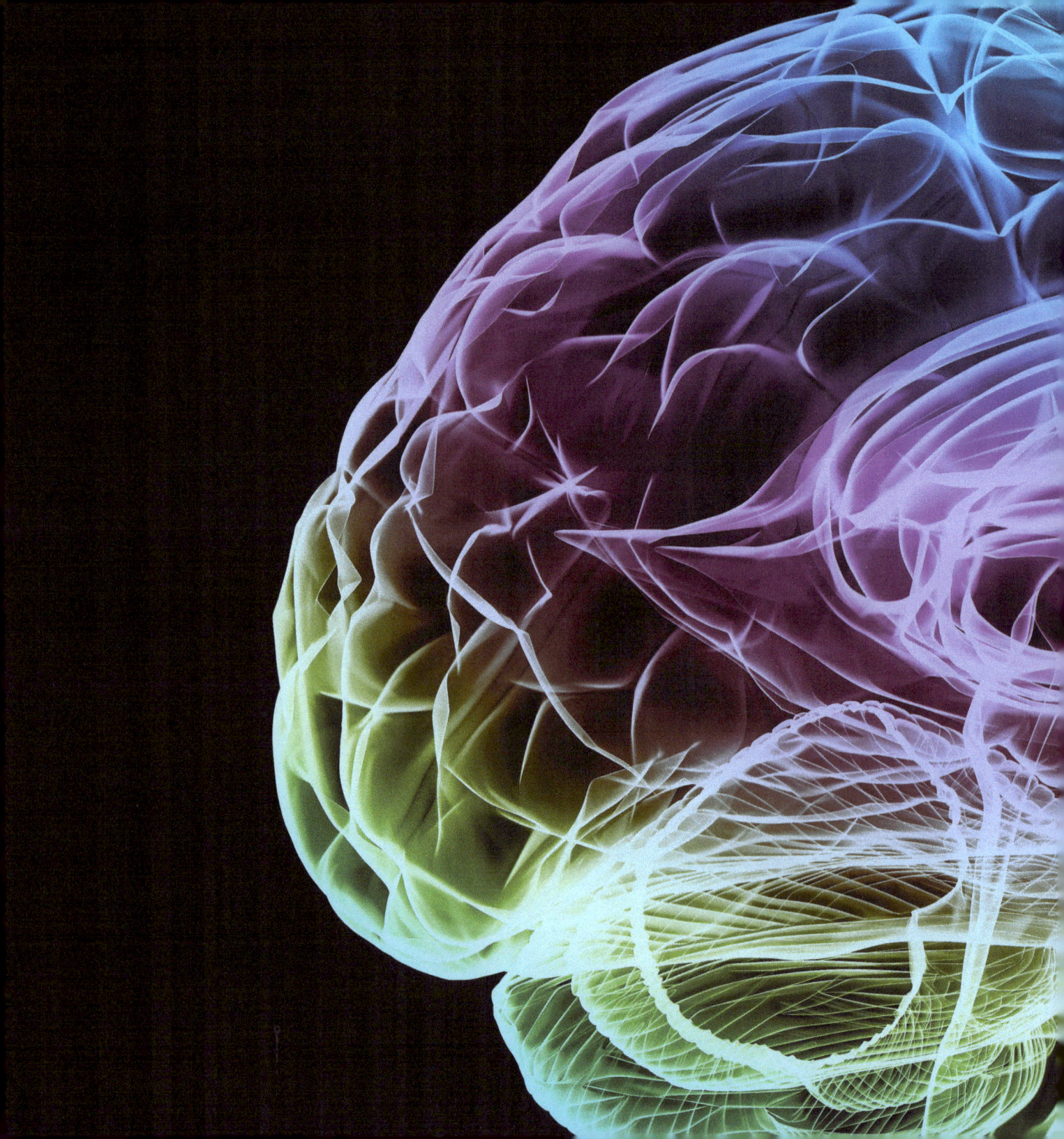

Your brain is the control center of your body. Through the nervous system, the brain receives information from our senses (sight, hearing, taste, smell, and touch) and from our organs, and sends signals to direct our organs.

Our brain allows us to think and learn. It is the controller of our body. All the vital daily functions like digestion, breathing and heart rate are controlled by our brain.

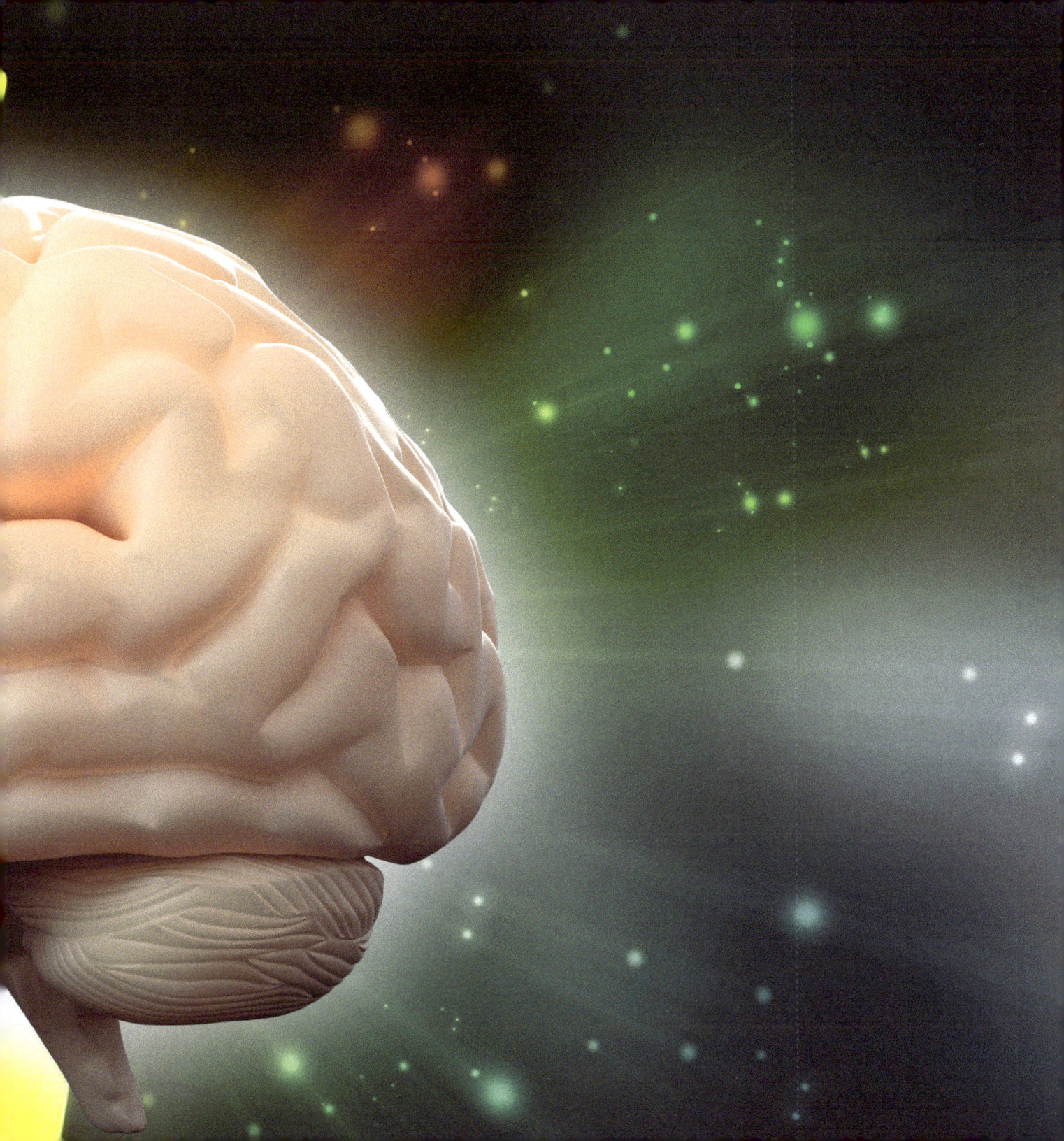

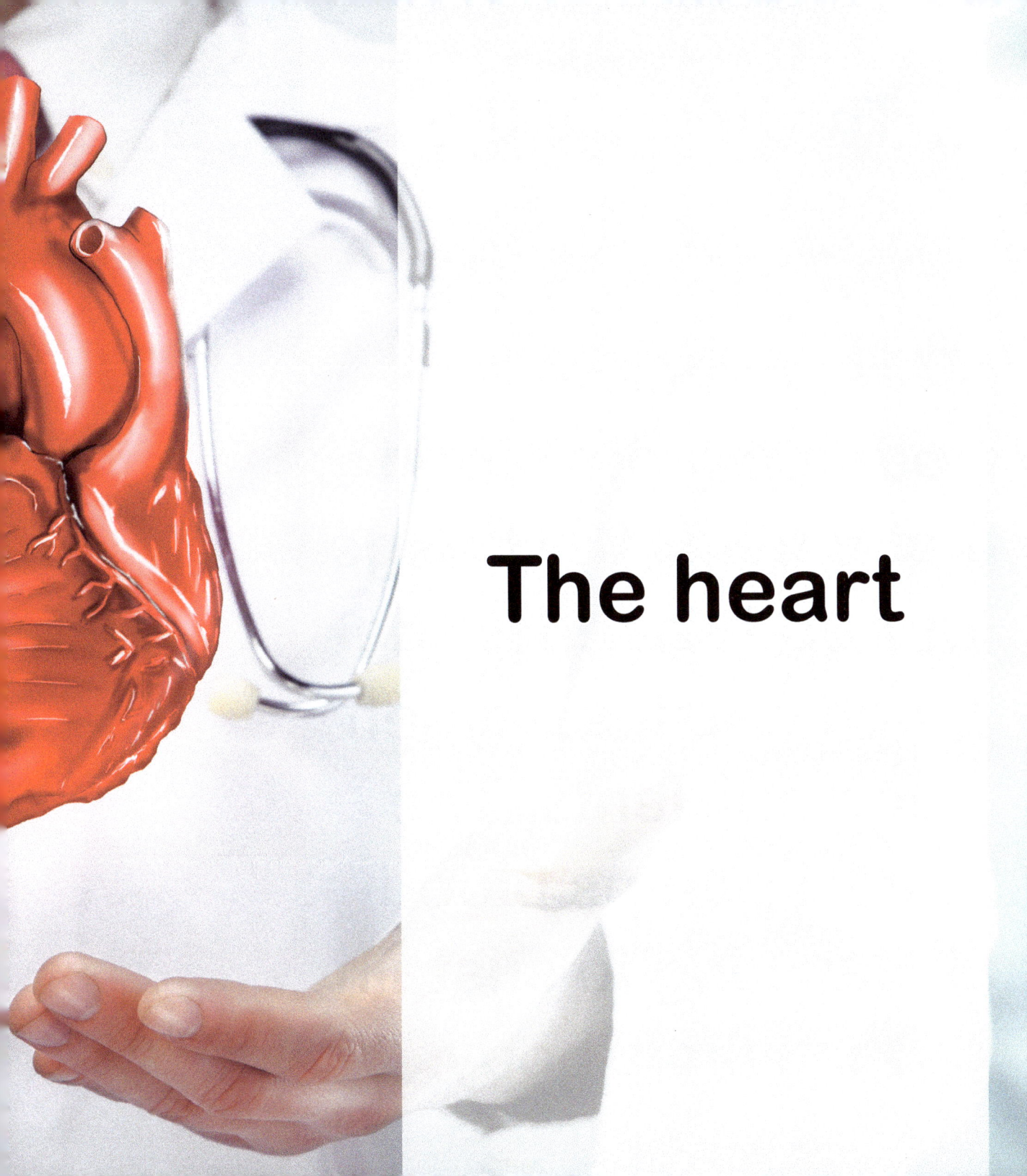

The heart

The heart is the centerpiece of life. The heart is responsible for pumping the blood that carries the things our body needs. The blood carries oxygen and nutrients. The heart pumps blood all day long to sustain the whole body.

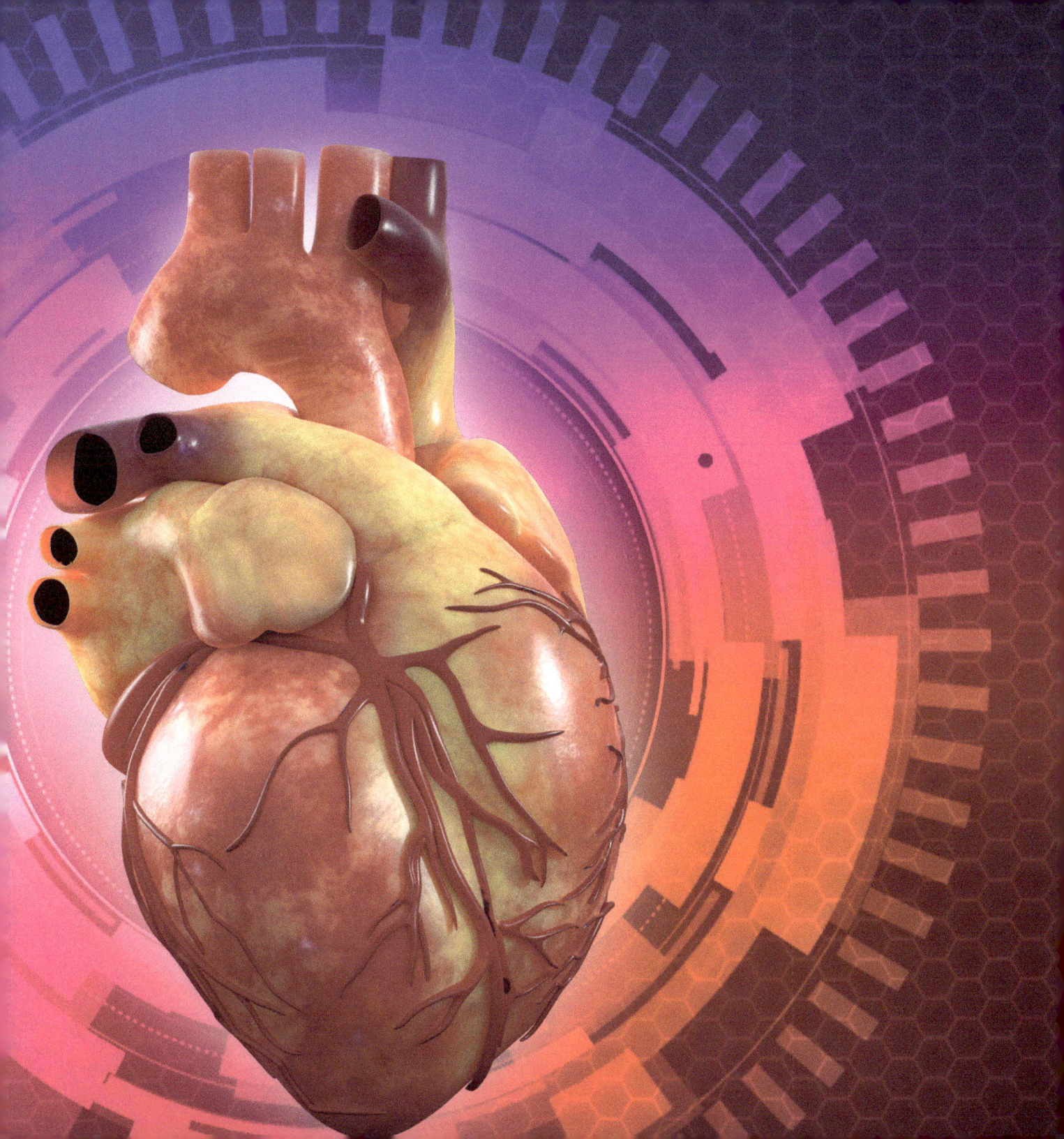

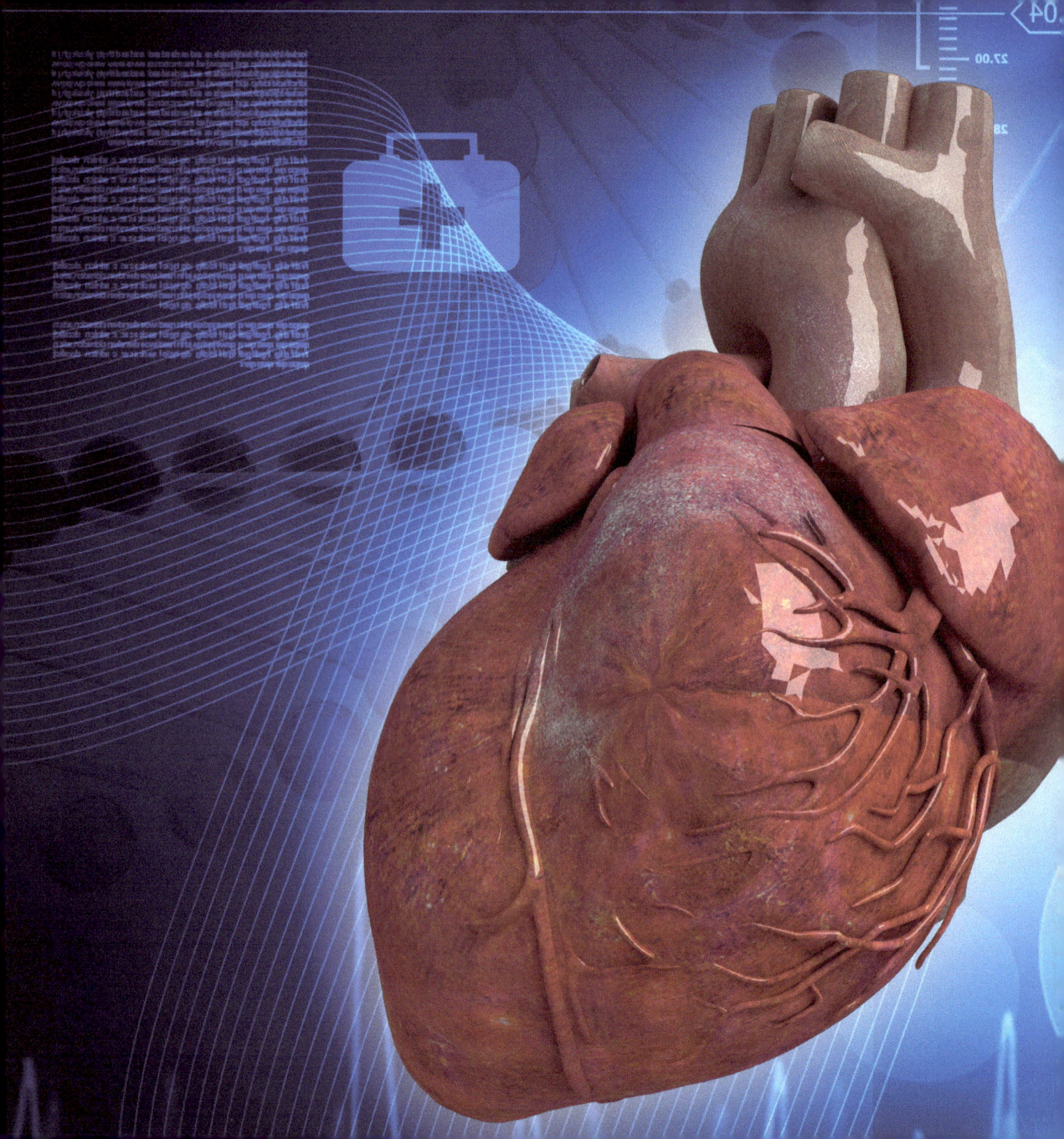

The heart should function well so we can live longer and have good health. That is why medical professionals usually measure our heart rate. This is a vital statistic.

The kidneys

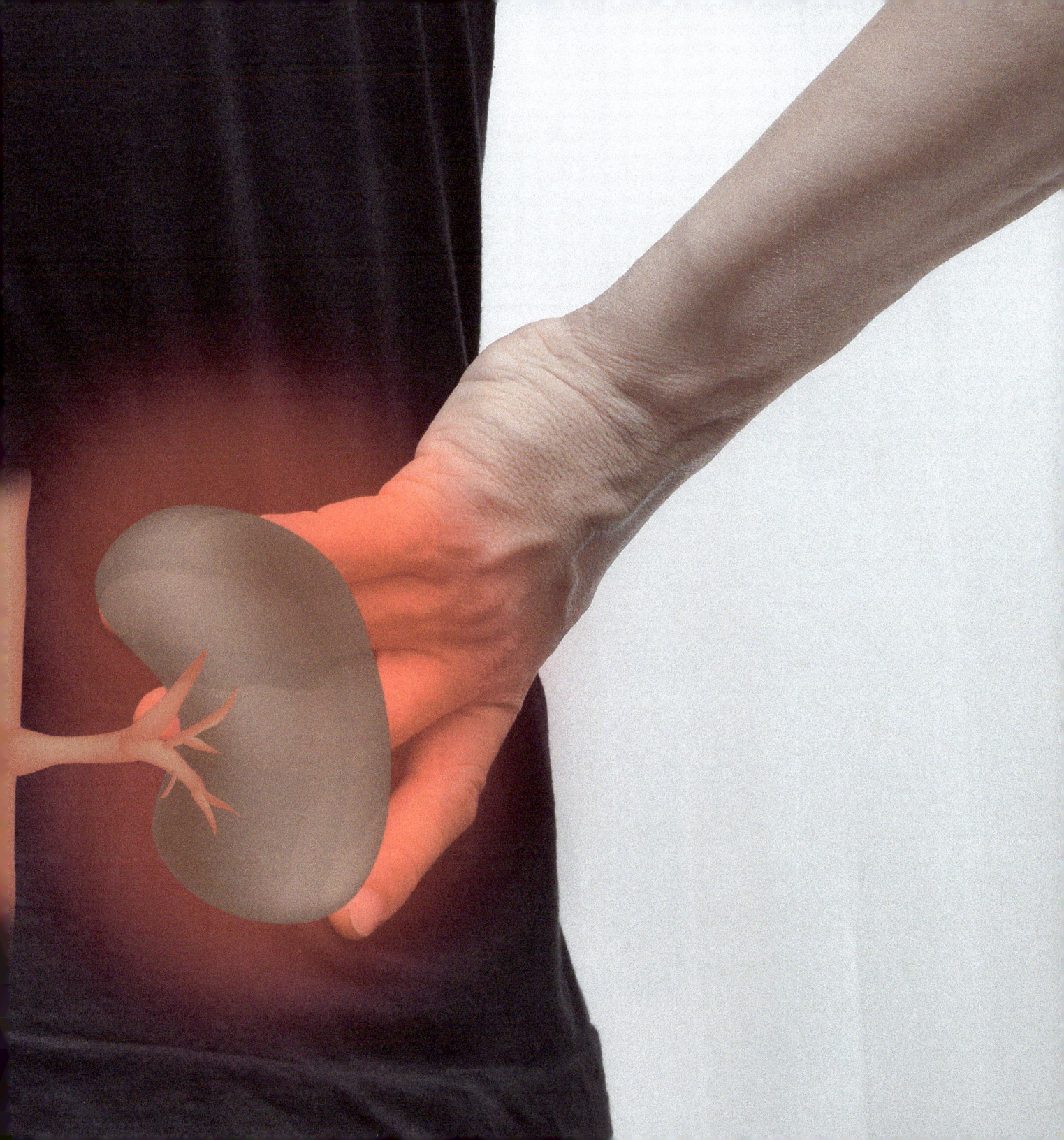

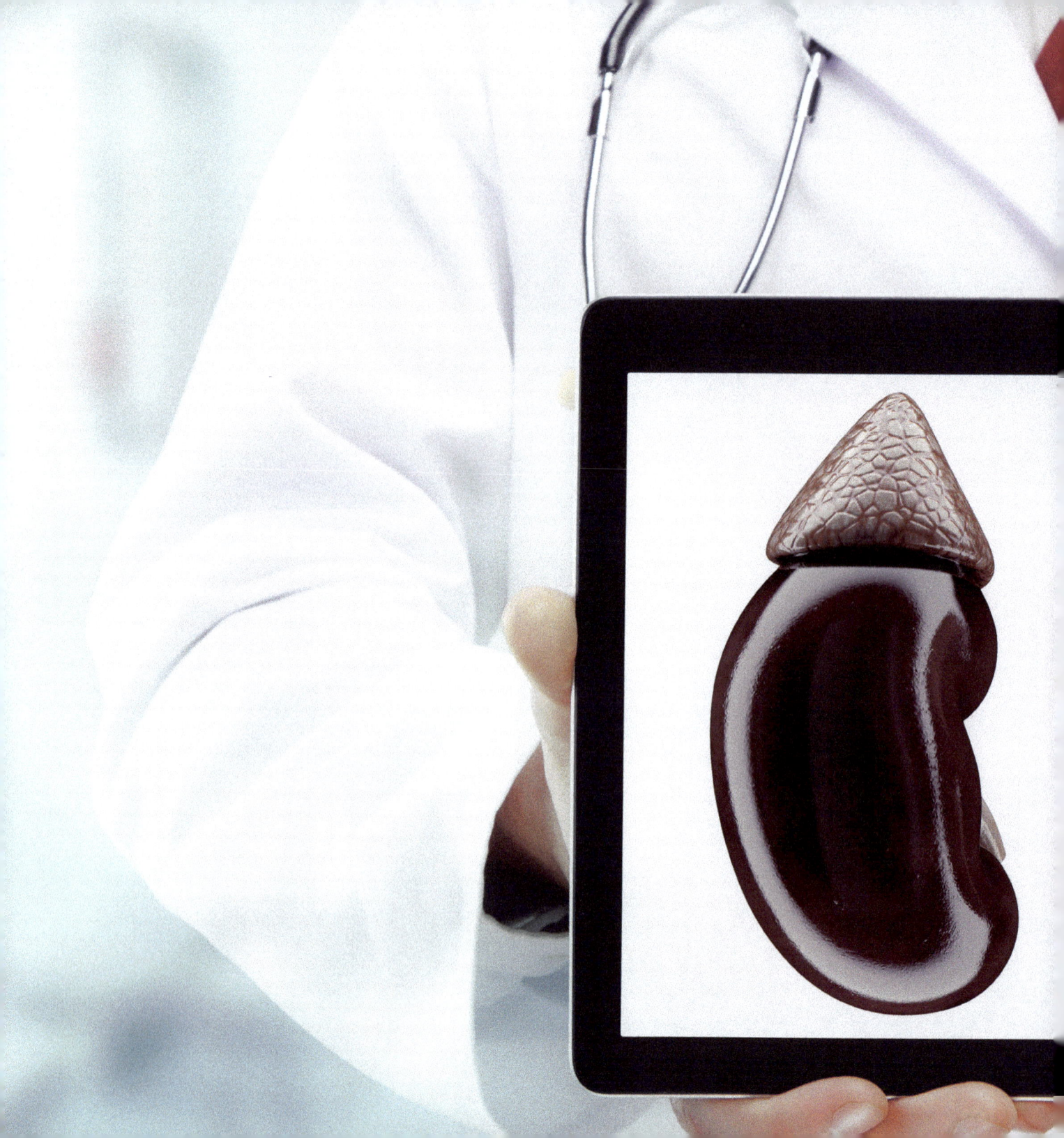

Our kidneys perform a very important role in our body. They are found under the ribcage in our lower back. The kidneys are responsible for removing waste and extra fluids from our blood.

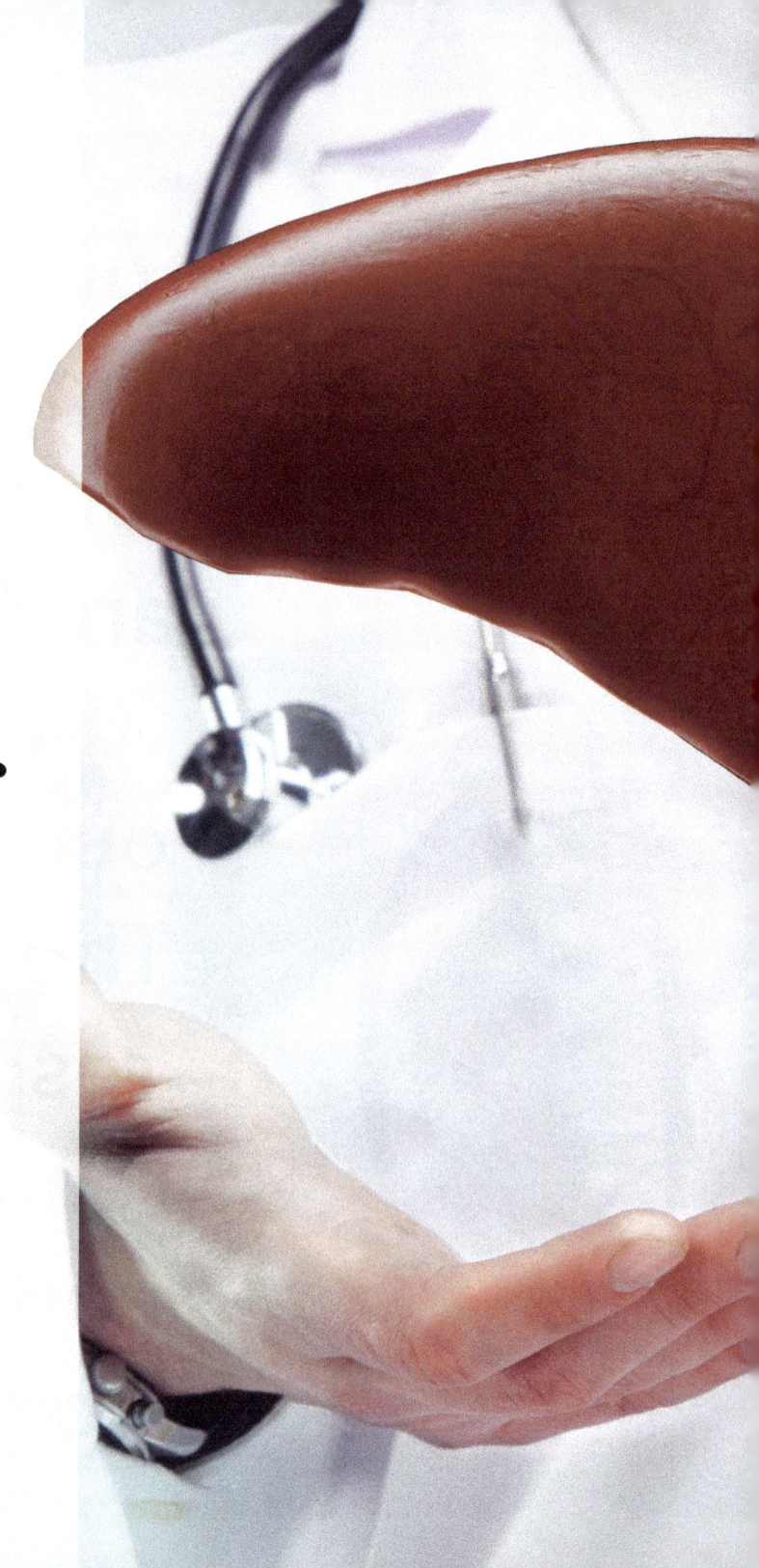

The liver

The liver is the largest internal organ. Our liver is situated in the upper abdomen, slightly to the left side. Its main role is to produce bile, which is sent to the stomach to help digest our food.

The liver detoxifies harmful chemicals. It also regulates our blood sugar. It releases cholesterol, breaks down fats and produces blood proteins.

26.85

46.158

38.42

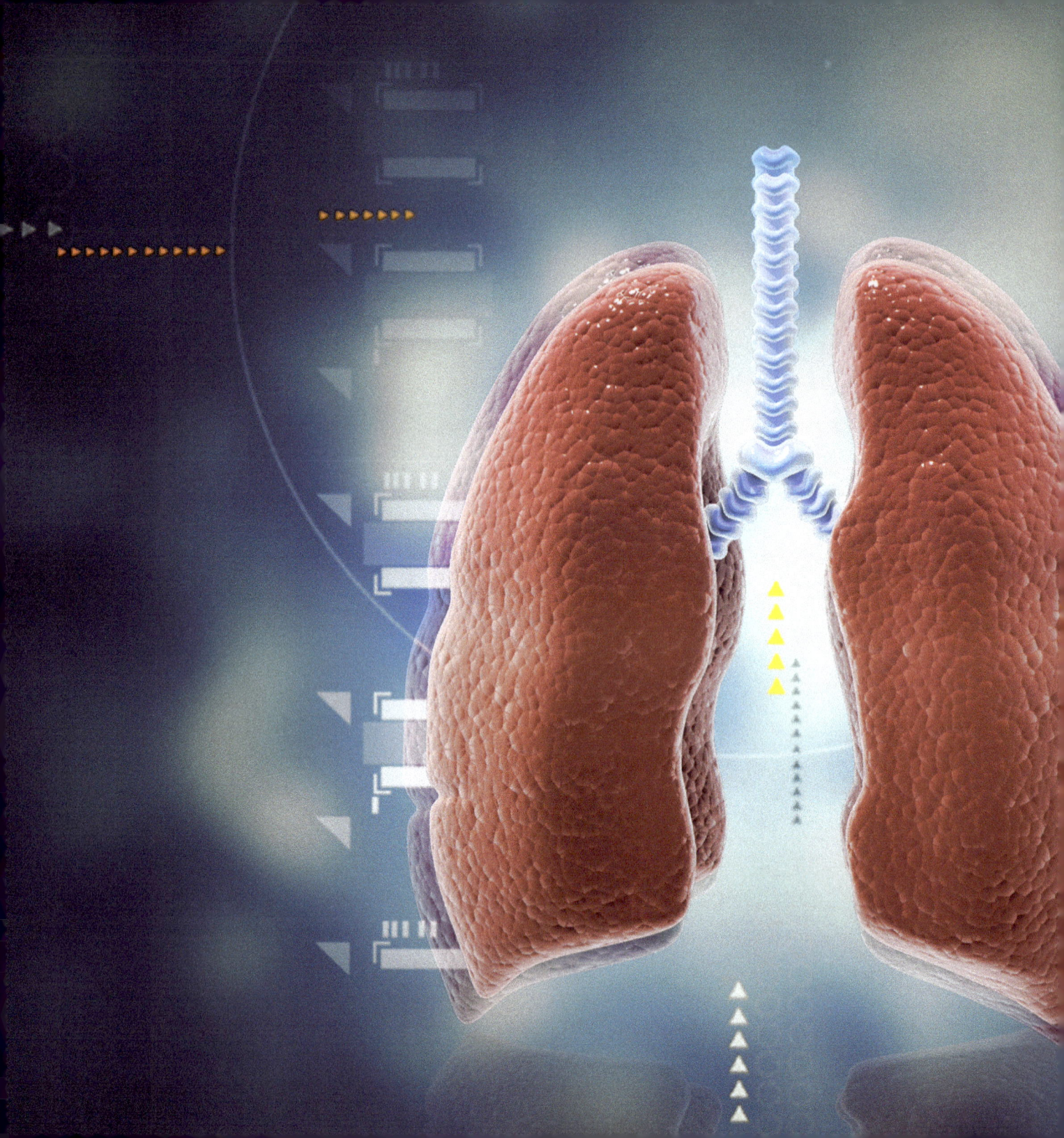

The lungs

Our breathing rate is another vital statistic. We breathe in to take in fresh air and breathe out to release gas we cannot use. We cannot live without breathing, so our lungs are considered key organs.

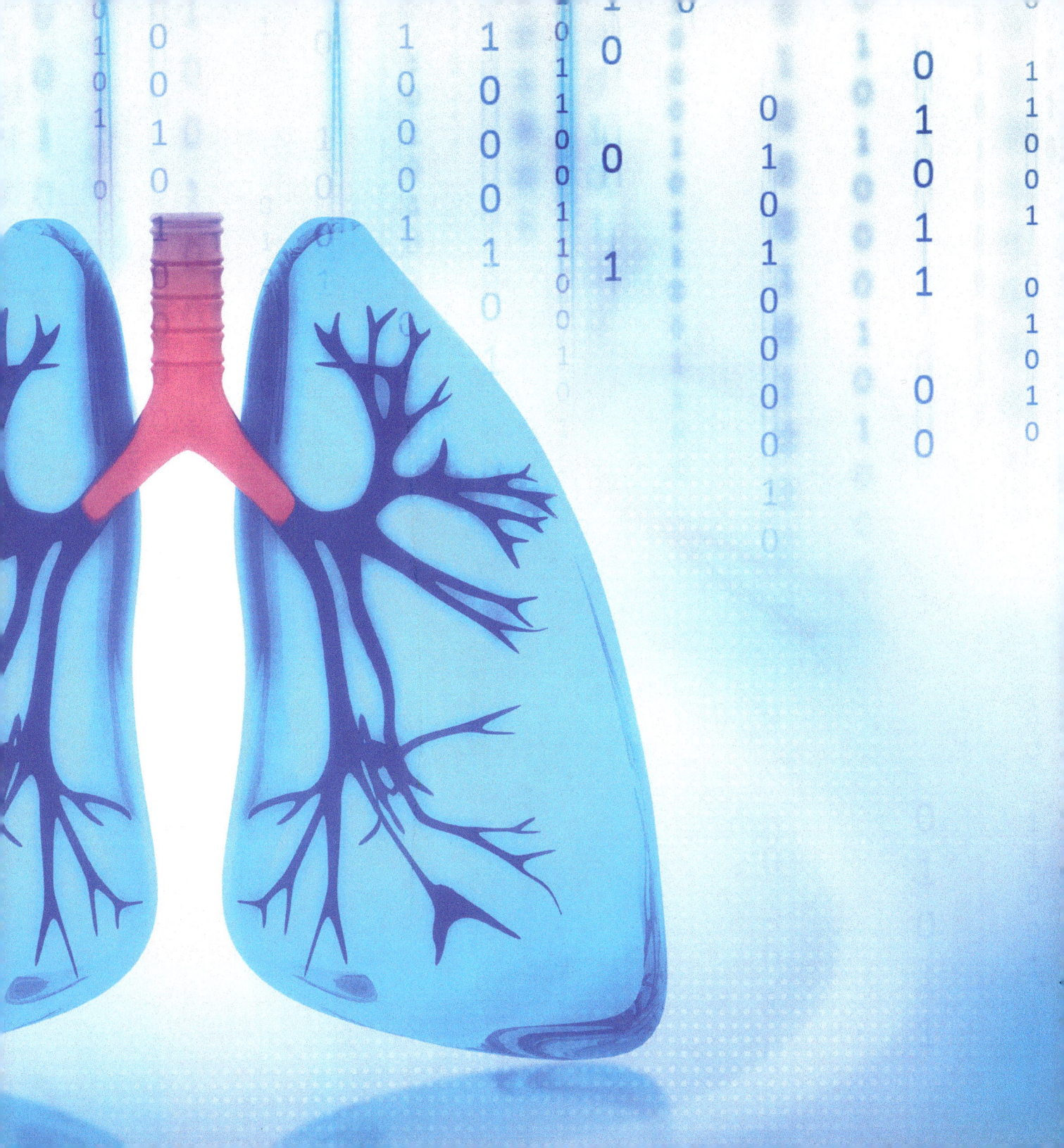

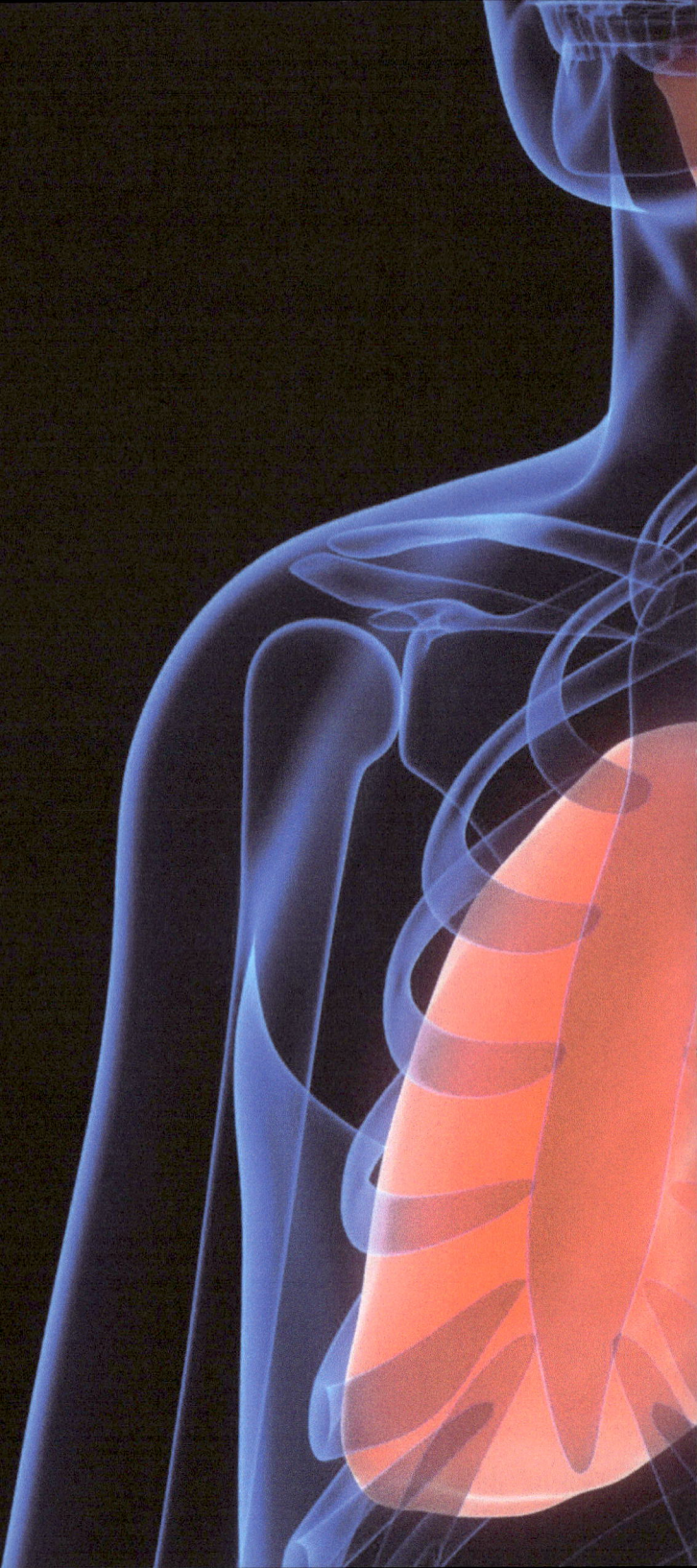

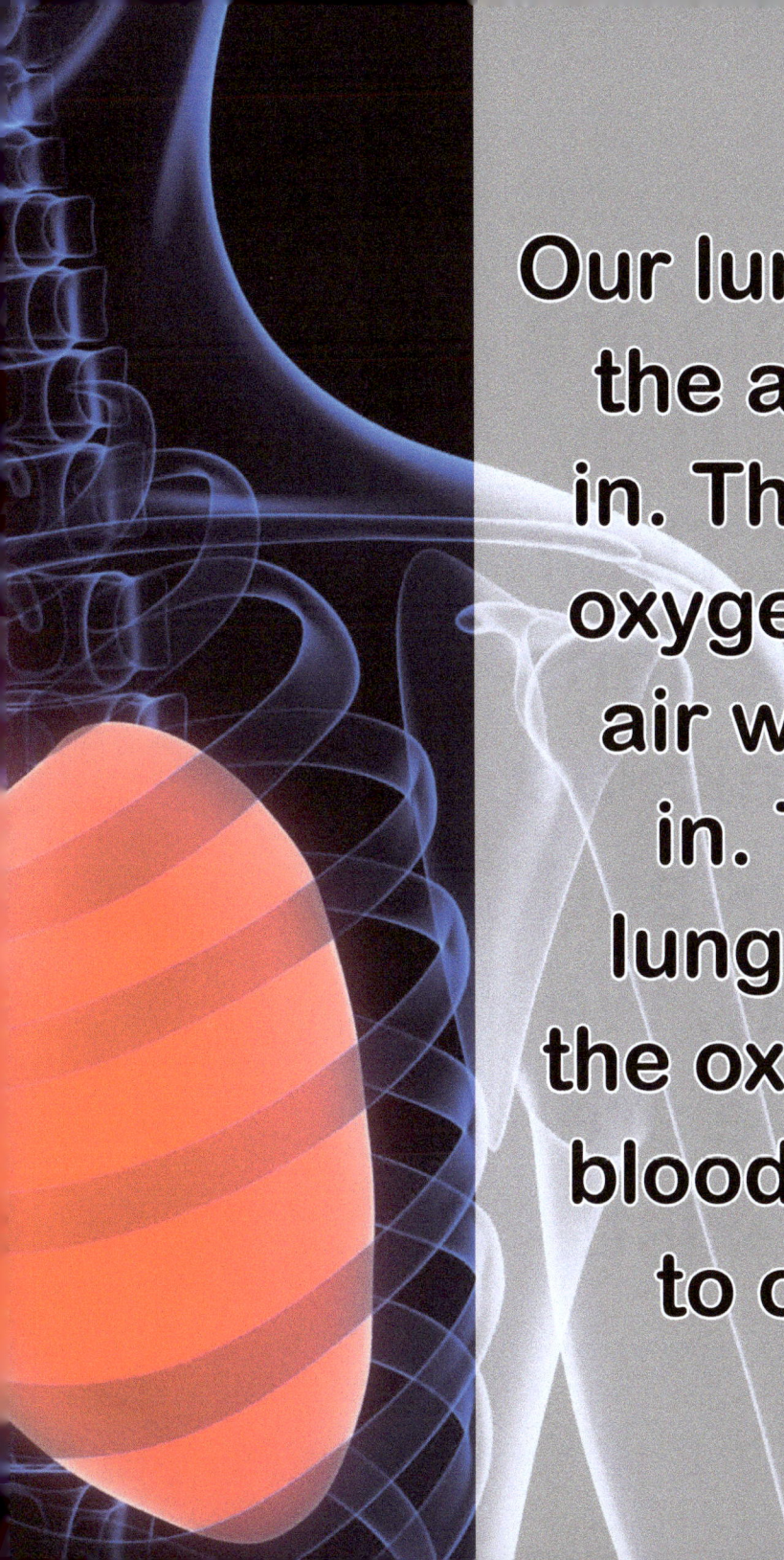

Our lungs process the air we take in. They remove oxygen from the air we breathe in. Then the lungs transfer the oxygen to our blood to be sent to our cells.

These organs are really vital. They help us live. Their specific functions are what make us able to think and run and play. We breathe! We are alive! We exist!

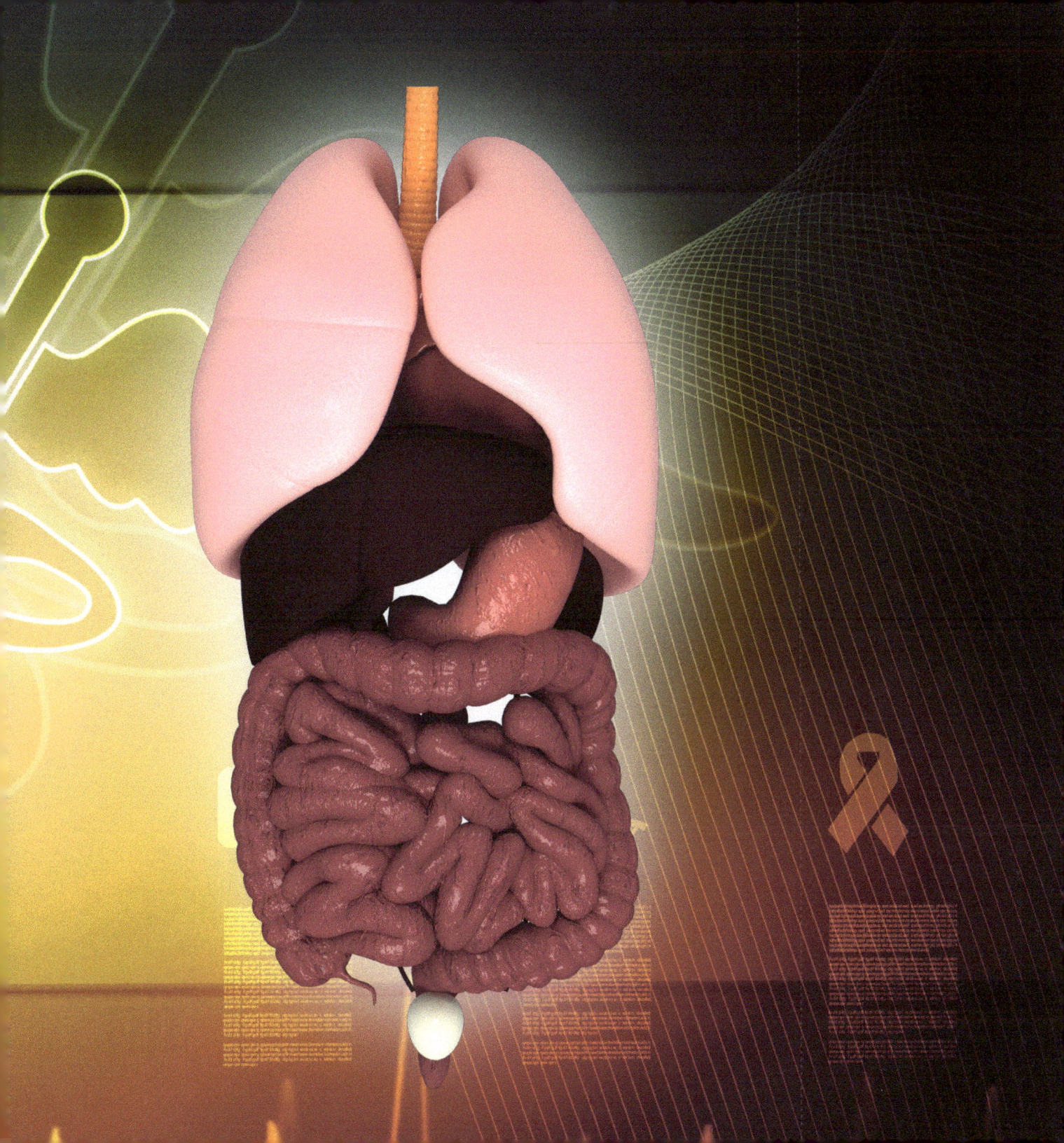

Milton Keynes UK
Ingram Content Group UK Ltd.
UKHW051456160124
436126UK00016B/803